King
for a
Day

by Meish Goldish

illustrated by
Hrana Janto

Scott Foresman

Editorial Offices: Glenview, Illinois • New York, New York
Sales Offices: Reading, Massachusetts • Duluth, Georgia
Glenview, Illinois • Carrollton, Texas • Menlo Park, California

Long ago, in a land far away, lived a king and queen. They were a very truthful couple. They never told a lie.

Indeed, the king and queen could not lie, even if they tried. In this land, a Truth Keeper ruled over them. The Truth Keeper made sure that what the royal couple said was always true.

One day, the king and queen went to a festival. Before they left, they spoke to their son, the prince.

"We will be back tomorrow," they told him. "You will rule here until then. All will go well if you just tell the truth."

They kissed the prince and got into their carriage. Then they were off.

The prince sat down to eat his breakfast. "Mmmm, these biscuits look good," he thought. Just then a heavy rain began to pound the castle walls.

"Listen to that!" the prince cried. "It is raining cats and dogs outside!"

Suddenly, the rain stopped and in its place, he heard a strange, new noise. It sounded terrible!

Falling from the sky were barking dogs and meowing cats!

"What *is* this?" The prince forgot all about his biscuits.

Suddenly a lady stood before him. Her clothes were rumpled and wrinkled. The prince stared. Who was she?

"I am the Truth Keeper," she said. "You said it was raining cats and dogs. Since a king must never lie, what you said must be true."

"I didn't mean that," the prince said. "I only meant that it was raining hard."

"It's what you say that counts," the Truth Keeper replied. She smoothed her rumpled skirt. Then she nibbled on a biscuit.

The prince couldn't believe it. "Is this a joke?" he asked. "You must be pulling my leg."

And in an instant, she was!

"Let go!" the prince ordered. "Cut it out!"

The Truth Keeper took out a large pair of scissors. The prince quickly thought about his words.

"I mean stop it!" he cried. "Put those scissors away and stop it from raining— anything!"

And so she did.

Dogs chased cats over the castle wall.

"Prince!" the servants cried. "Dogs and cats are filling up the castle! You must do something. Right now!"

The prince needed time to think. "Just hold your horses," he told them.

Suddenly, horses filled the castle yard.
They reared up and kicked their feet high.

The prince quickly made a plan. "Catch all
the dogs and cats now," he said.

"But we cannot," the servants said. "For the
truth is, we are afraid of dogs and cats."

"Afraid of dogs and cats?" the prince cried.
"Then you are all nothing but chickens!"

Suddenly, piles of wrinkled, rumpled clothes littered the yard. The servants were gone. Instead, chickens ran in circles. Cats chased the chickens. Dogs chased the cats. Horses chased the dogs.

"Oh, no!" The prince groaned. "Truth Keeper, please! Tell me what to do!"

The Truth Keeper stood before him. "You must catch all the animals yourself," she said.

"But they're everywhere!" the prince cried. "You're sending me on a wild goose chase!"

Of course, dozens of geese appeared.

The prince sat down and shook his head in misery.

"Oh, Truth Keeper," he cried. "Look at the mess I've made! I've failed. I guess I'm just not a very good ruler. It makes me so sad. I really am down in the dumps."

Suddenly, the prince smelled something very bad. He looked up. He was sitting on garbage!

"Where *am* I?" he cried.

"You're down in the dumps," the Truth Keeper replied.

"Well, let's get out of here," the prince said. He wrinkled his nose. "This place smells. And that's the truth!"

The prince and the Truth Keeper spent the whole night catching animals.

The prince said he was sorry he had called his servants chickens. In an instant, the chickens turned back into servants.

By the time the sun rose, all was back in order.

Soon the king and queen returned from the festival.

"How did things go while we were gone?" they asked. "Did you always tell the truth?"

"Yes, I did," the prince said. He reached for the plate of biscuits. Then he bit into a biscuit.

"Mmmm," he cried. "These biscuits are *out of this world*!"